Val McDermid ∾ Arthur Robins

My Granny
is a
PIRATE

For Cameron, without whom
this would not have happened – V.McD.

For Katie and Olivia, with love – A.R.

ORCHARD BOOKS
338 Euston Road, London NW1 3BH
Orchard Books Australia
Level 17/207 Kent Street, Sydney, NSW 2000

First published in 2012 by Orchard Books
First paperback publication in 2012

ISBN 978 1 40830 927 8

Text © Val McDermid 2012
Illustrations © Arthur Robins 2012

The rights of Val McDermid to be identified as the author
and of Arthur Robins to be identified as the illustrator
of this work have been asserted by them in accordance
with the Copyright, Designs and Patents Act, 1988.

A CIP catalogue record for this book is available from the British Library.

7 9 10 8 6

Printed in China

Orchard Books is a division of Hachette Children's Books,
an Hachette UK Company.

www.hachette.co.uk

Val McDermid ∽ Arthur Robins
My Granny
is a
PIRATE

ORCHARD

My family has a secret
I'm not allowed to tell.
They'd chase me if I told you
And then chase you as well.

So, if I share the secret
You've got to keep it too.
Just swear upon this gold doubloon
And then I can trust you.

HERE'S THE SECRET . . .

My granny is a PIRATE!
She's sailed the seven seas.

She captured many pirate ships
But was always home for tea.

She started as a cabin girl.
She climbed the rigging high,

And called out to the crew below
When treasure ships she'd spy.

She was so fierce in battle
Her reputation grew.
Soon every other pirate feared
She'd capture their ship too.

She kept a pirate parrot
Who whistled, talked and danced.

His antics were remarkable –
They kept the crew entranced.

My granny is a pirate!
She's sailed the ocean blue.
She's captured many pirate ships

And many pirate crews.

She made them swab her decks.

She made them walk the plank.

She made them carry pirate gold
Back to the pirate bank.

She loved to sing sea shanties
And walk her pirate dog.

She called him
JOLLY ROGER

And fed him pirate grog!

Each evening, after sunset,
They anchored in the bay.
She gave the crew their orders
And then she slipped away.

She took her pirate rowboat
And headed for the shore
Without a single splash from
Her wooden pirate oars.

Inside a deep, dark cavern,
Her granny clothes she'd keep.
She'd change and grab her handbag,
Climb the secret passage steep
That wound up through the hillside
To the ruined castle keep.

BUT . . .

Wherever there are ruins,
You'll find some spooky ghouls,

Some skeletons
and ghosties

And creepy
things that drool.

Wherever there are pirates,
There's treasure near at hand.

So, the skeletons decided
To form a robber band.

So, down the secret passage
Came bony spooks and hags
And up the secret passage . . .

Came Granny with her bag!

They met right in the middle,
The skeletons and Gran.
The parrot squawked in terror . . .

And then the fight began!

She threw her handbag at them
Without a second thought.
The skeletons were broken up
Before they even fought.

The best bones they were taken
By Granny's pirate dog.

They celebrated victory
With mugs of pirate grog.

Yes, Granny is a pirate!
I'm telling you it's true!
And if I keep her secret
(she's promised, if I keep it)
Yes, if I keep her secret

I can be a pirate too.